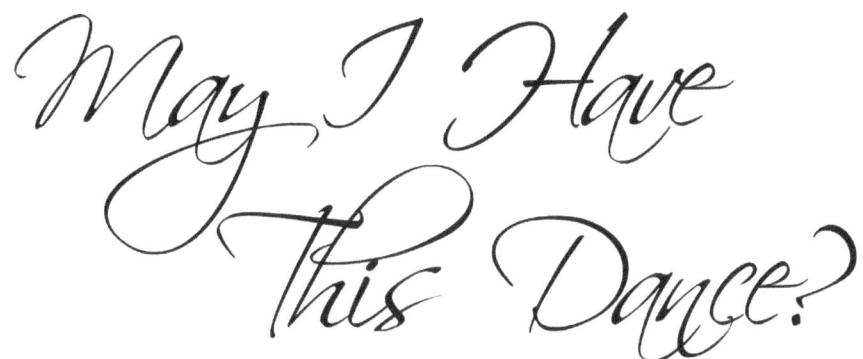

Sue M. Hodkinson

Ocala, FL

Copyright © 2007, 2018 Sue Hodkinson

All rights reserved. No part of this publication may be reproduced, distributed, or transmitted in any form or by any means, including photocopying, recording, or other electronic or mechanical methods, without the prior written permission of the publisher, except in the case of brief quotations embodied in critical reviews and certain other noncommercial uses permitted by copyright law. For permission requests, write to the publisher, addressed "Attention: Permissions Coordinator," at the address below.

Zeta Publishing, Inc
3850 SE 58th Ave
Ocala, FL 34480
www.zetapublishing.com

The views expressed in this work are solely those of the author and do not necessarily reflect the views of the publisher, and the publisher hereby disclaims any responsibility for them.

Ordering Information:
Quantity sales. Special discounts are available on quantity purchases by corporations, associations, and others. For details, contact the publisher at the address above. Orders by U.S. trade bookstores and wholesalers. Please contact Zeta Publishing: Tel: (352) 694-2553; Fax: (352) 694-1791 or visit www.zetapublishing.com

First Published by

Rev. Date: July 2018

ISBN: 978-1-947191-90-7 (sc)

ISBN: 978-1-947191-91-4 (e)

Library of Congress Control Number: 2018949138

Printed in the United States of America

Dedication

My Father, I came running and You opened Your arms with a tender embrace to secure me, and in that very awesome moment, my life was changed.

It is written in **First Corinthians 2: 9-13:** *"No eye has seen, nor ear has heard, nor mind has conceived what God has prepared for those who love Him. God has revealed it to us by His Spirit. The spirit searches all things even the deep things of God. We have not received the spirit of the world, but the spirit who is from God that we may understand what God has freely given us. We speak what we speak, not in words taught us by human wisdom, but in words taught by the Spirit of God, expressing spiritual truths in spiritual words."* These attributes, embroideries, and trinkets of my soul are an eloquence of multicolored rainbows, adorned with fabric straight from the Master's hand. Gifts imparted through the emotions of my heart, of moments past, given in flames of passion—ever glowing to glorify His love and devotion of the dance. Thank you for choosing me! I set this work apart just for you. Let the music play!

Foreword

Jesus said to them: "Come away by yourselves to a secluded place and rest awhile." (Mark 6:31)NIV

As a Pastor, among the many blessings I have received from God, are the friends I have made along the way. I first met Sue about three years ago as she joined our congregation. It did not take long at all to develop a close relationship with her in, no small part, due to her complete openness about her relationship with her Father: God. To say she is enthusiastic about Jesus would be a complete understatement. She radiates exuberance which is definitely catching. I believe one of her fervent prayers for all of us is to have a close and loving relationship with the one who loves us beyond what we can know with our intellect, but rather what we treasure in our hearts. We desire to be loved. We desire to have that peace in our souls that can only come when we are sure that the object of our desire is just as passionate for us as we for Him. That kind of relationship takes time to develop, and it takes understanding. In this day with all our cares, concerns, and distractions, we sometime forget to set aside that time when we can remember our first love, our first embrace, our first encounter with a God whose desire for us is to know Him with all of our heart and soul. In *"May I Have this Dance?"* Sue uses an invitation to the dance to illustrate the joy and peace that come from knowing that God will ask to be close to us, and invite us into a relationship with Him. All we need to do is respond. He is patient, kind, and full of grace; willing to meet us wherever we are. We just need to answer yes, when He asks us to join Him in the dance. Take your time and meditate on this invitation. Do not be timid, rather a willing participant. In my memory of dancing, I am the person with two left feet who would rather sit and watch instead of joining. I remember one time many years ago, being at a dance where my wife's cousin, Rita was in attendance. Rita is a dance instructor and managed to coax me onto the dance floor. I was unconfident, fearful that I would step on her feet or worse. She assured me all would be alright and just to follow her lead. I thought, the man should be leading, but rather than being stubborn, I took her advice, relaxed, and followed. Before I realized it, I was dancing, and I was enjoying it. Our God wants to fill us with joy! He wants to be close to us and give us all our desires. He wants us to live to the fullest. He wants us to desire Him as much as He desires us. He has extended His hand, and all you have to do is say: "Yes, Lord, it will be my pleasure to join You!" Do not just watch from the side, but participate in the celebration. Do not be timid, but accepting. The orchestra is playing your song! The time is NOW! The Master is calling and the choice is yours—"Shall you dance?"

Father Chuck Dixon+
St. Michael the Archangel Church
54 Cardinal Ave. Rockledge, FL. 32955

Introduction

Can you imagine dancing with God in preparation for the experience heaven will bring? This is not a carnal or physical attraction by the world's definition, but a wooing, a spiritual longing of the heart—a living expression of His song and dance. His melody is pure, simple, and exclusive to His touch. Our joys, sorrows, and aspirations are created by His own hand to lead us with enthusiasm into His promises and eternal song. Look to the skyline, the horizon of your soul.

Psalms 51:11 cries: "Cast me not away from thy presence. *(My cry is: "But dance with me, My King!")* ***Banish me not from thy house and ordinances.*** *(My cry is: "Living the way of the world denies us the sent one, Jesus Christ, our Savior, and the cross, the deliverer of our salvation. You are the answer!")* ***Take not thy Holy Spirit from me."*** *(My cry is: "But journey with me! Life encourages us to engage the path the world would have us take. Each path may look right, but there is only one path that leads to life.")* Knowing these truths, I cannot justify the sin that dwells within, nor the departure of Your Spirit forever, as such are the consequences of sin, along with the depth of its power until death. Turn not thy face from me, nor abandon me to Hell's termination. Stay with me so that I may call you my King! Do not take Your *saving grace* from me. My request is to embrace me! Dance with me through the heartbreaks of life. Dance with me through my iniquity, and the creative darkness of my soul. Be the light at the edge of my darkest hour! My sin, my sorrow, my delay, and my denial are against You, my King, and You alone! My search for the dance brings the consolation of knowing my redemption draws nigh as my Savior approaches with an eternal flame and a mission that will secure my life before Him in eternity—forever victorious as my Savior and my King!

Therefore, let us:

"Pick up the golden chalice to walk through the open door,
Don't look back His children; He has your best in store.
The Maestro makes ready, not destiny by chance;
Hand in hand His children, "May He indeed have this dance?"
Step lightly to the music; He will guide the notes,
A symphony of splendor as He creates the strokes.
Glide across the dance floor; His melody is known.
Don't be shy His children; His will to you is shown.
Look up into the heavens; His melody is about your feet.
No time for indecision; you must not take a seat.
His hand is far extended; the moment has arrived,
Thus for you intended; He orchestrates this tide!"

After the climax of music has played its course, turn to your Heavenly Father at the end of the dance and give Him your courtesy bow! The time is NOW, and the King is waiting! You will not regret it!

WHAT OTHERS ARE SAYING ABOUT
SUE HODKINSON
AND
"May I Have This Dance?"

"An inspired beautiful reminder to the Bride of Christ of His great love for us!"
— **Florence Lewis, Titusville, FL. 32780**

"An excellent example of one's love of our Holy Father, GOD. Sue's written words will help us to truly understand how one can have an open loving, and faithful relationship with our Father ourselves. The book reminded me of the movie "Forest Gump," where life is like a box of chocolates. When turning the pages, I did not know which flavor I would experience next. I'd recommend every Christian have this book on their shelf!"
— **Dale & Debi Hopper, Titusville, FL. 32780**

"May I Have This Dance?" is a beautifully written book about intimacy, and a desire to go to a closeness that only the Father orchestrates. If there is no height, nor depth to His love, then what are we waiting for? Eternity with our Lord is one dance to which we should all want to respond. Sue Hodkinson has captured a level of God's heart that cannot be denied. God will plant joyful

splendor in your heart that will be germinated by the warmth of His love for you!"

— **James & Lindsey Ristow, Titusville, FL. 32780**

"A pebble thrown into a pool is an ever widening, never ending circle of continued joy experienced in this oracle of the writer. However, to the reader "May I Have this Dance?" is profound. This magnificent flowing book is a fervent needed rescue for souls that think they have no rhythm for God's dance. ***"May I Have this Dance?"*** *is a sublime, intimate instruction from The Master to the soul's delight. BRAVO to the Mighty King! Place this on your night table. Keep it there for enlightenment and reflected peace. A ten star review!"*

— **T. J. Kelly, Space Coast area, FL.**

"Thou hast made us for thyself, O Lord, and our heart is restless until it finds its rest in thee." St. Augustine of Hippo 354-430 ***"May I Have this Dance?"*** *paints such a beautiful image in your mind of the love, and joy that can be yours when you let the Lord lead you."*

— **Siobhan Wright, Mims, FL.**

"The author gives us a deep appreciation for what it truly means to love God. As Jesus tells us in the gospel of **Matthew 22:37:** *"The great, and first commandment is to love the Lord your God with all you heart, and with all your soul, and with all your mind."* ***"May I Have this Dance?"*** *will leave you with an insight on how deep, and complete that love can be."*

— **Wade Wright, Mims, FL.**

"Each word, each phrase, each page, left me sensing my own heart beat within my chest. My mind was flashing images of my Creator pursuing, wooing, and searching for His chosen beloved creation. The words, and images leapt from the pages; stirring a desire to truly experience, create, and become all that He has placed inside of me to become. Her words sparked a deep desire to experience all that is written. The book leaves the reader with much to consider as we each journey through the seasons of our lives. Sue's writing's remind us that God is pursuing us, wooing us with the same type of tenderness, and zeal that a young man employs when trying to win the heart of the woman he loves. **Song of Solomon 5:2 says: "I slept but my heart was awake, listen my lover is knocking!" Song of Solomon 2: 10-13 says: "My lover spoke and said to me: "Arise, My darling, My beautiful one, and come with Me. See the winter is past, the rains are gone; flowers appear on the earth. The season of singing has come!"** *Is this the season of your life when you also desire to accept His invitation? Can you hear the music? May I Have this Dance?"*

— ***Trena Tremblay, Rockledge, FL.***

"Sue captures the divine call of the Spirit to His people to enter into the bridal chamber. As you read it, let Him draw you into an intimate relationship with this Bridegroom King!"

— ***Pastor Roger Hackenburg, Hope Fellowship Church, Titusville, FL.***

"Don't just read this as a devotional, but let the Holy Spirit touch your spirit with the longings of the Father's heart. Sue M. Hodkinson has heard the heart of the Father, and leads you into the dance of Mahanaim—the place where Heaven and Earth touch!" **Song of Songs 6:13**
— **Pastor Dory Valley, Hope Fellowship Church, Titusville, FL., Women's Ministries**

"I know of nothing greater the Triune God desires than true intimacy with us. From this, flow every thought, word, and deed pleasing to Him, including our obedience to His will and the fulfillment of our purpose. Just as faith without works is dead, so servile obedience without an intimate, loving relationship bears little fruit. Always He calls, always He invites, always He whispers, as near as your very breath. Freefall into His waiting arms. You have nothing to fear and everything from now through eternity to gain."

— *Julie Wales, Cocoa, FL.*

"As I was reading "May I Have this Dance?" I could feel the Holy Spirit drawing me in and reaching out to me. It reminded me of the movie "The Shack", where I had to visualize the Trinity for me to understand what I was seeing. In Sue's book, I experienced the feeling the words created when I read them on paper. I kept trying to get there, but it was me trying instead of allowing the Holy Spirit to transport me."

— *Marilyn Coates, Cocoa, FL.*

"A myriad of individuals believe, pray, love and worship our one and only Father God. Yet, many are unaware that one's relationship with Him can evolve and delve into a much closer and more intimate relationship on a deeper plane if one seeks, desires, and expresses same to God. (I know this because prior to meeting Sue, I believed the "topical" relationship I had with my Heavenly Father was all that would exist until I met Him after my death.) "May I Have this Dance?" projects a profound awakening, and explicit portrayal of our Heavenly Father, and His response, and reciprocity with immense pleasure of yearning to make Him her entire world, and to place Him first as He desires. I can feel the anointing of the Holy Spirit descending upon me as I am fed from her words vividly describing her encounters, and banters with God. Are you famished and parched from this fleshy world? Are you ready and willing to give God your all? Do you desire that up-close and personal relationship with Him? Then, no longer merely dip your toes in the edge of the River of Life, but fully immerse yourself in the waters and follow God through the portal into His astounding and unimaginable glory! This book is proof-positive a MUST READ, and genuine journey reflecting an intimacy with God that is doubtlessly attainable."

— **Teresa McNeary, Merritt Island, Fl.**

My greatest desire is to know Him, His character, and His nature;
To see and observe Him with great intent: the person of God.
I wish to stand before Him—to focus on this one and only God,
With the desire in my heart to serve Him with all my love.

Revelation 3:20

Here I am! I stand at the door and knock.
If anyone hears My voice and opens the door,
I will come in and eat with him, and he with Me.

Song of Solomon 5:2
I slept but my heart was awake, listen my lover is knocking...

Song of Solomon 2: 10-13
"My lover spoke and said to me, Arise My darling,
My beautiful one and come with Me.
See the winter is past, the rains are gone, flowers
appear on the earth. The season of singing has come!"

I am the Rose of Sharon. Quickly My love, arise and come to the falls, to the springtime of our love. The tranquility of our garden calls. Whither thou goest, My love, I will go. Behold a day's journey, a season of time, a devoted way of life; a paradise enclosed, a model of perfection, a state of bliss. I will read to you a sonnet, My love, to refresh your mood, to comfort, to please, to awaken, and to bring joy to your spirit. Look just ahead at the sunrise! This is a special gathering of time with all its many fragments, secured within My reach—coalesce, united into a single whole before Me.

Sue Hodkinson

Springtime is at its budding stage. You are a bud of distinction ready to blossom with the fullness of time. Be still, and listen for the cooing of the doves nesting. Each brook dances as the water trickles in sequence to the melody of our hearts' desire. Our song is distinctly heard about the nestling of the trees. There am I in the midst of our love. May I step out to embrace you for such a time as this—for a silhouette of light to shine upon our profile? I have orchestrated our song just for us. I can hear its harmony already My love, can you? You desire the softness of My touch. Peace be still; I will come! Peace be still; I will gather you! Peace be still! I am enclosing each moment collectively as time will rest. Yield to My pleasure over you. I am coming to knock on the door of your heart. Now, let Me in!

"My King, I am Your heart's desire. My thoughts of You are on tender display. You are a gallant knight on a solid white horse charging the enemies of my existence. A powerful steed of great might, and devotion, exercising Your authority to rule and to reign over my inheritance.

Behold! You are a flaming torch, an arrow in flight, a sign of Your superiority and power. How brilliantly Your shine halos our betrothal! I desire You, and the tranquility of Your presence. The smell of Your fragrance is so rich and pure. You are the atmosphere composed deep within my soul.

Unlock its chamber and embrace me. I wish to surrender all that I am. My gifts to You are Your very own.

Sue Hodkinson

"May I have this dance, My love? This is a special waltz, an arrangement I have orchestrated just for us. The sound and crest of its music are valuable to you so play each note wisely. Are you open to receive Me? If so, express your thoughts to Me, and I will listen for your impression. Searching, I saw you and felt the sincerity of your love for Me. I want to embrace you, and impart knowledge to be engraved upon the tablet of your heart. You need only come to Me.

My King! I hear the sound of abundance! The curtain is about to rise!

It is imperative that I lead, so take My hand and look into My eyes. In doing so, we will begin to flow together. You are a diamond of excellence, My love. A nugget in the rough whose karat cannot be compared. It's like a million lights caressing each other. You are My flower of preference and fragrance of choice. My desire is to have you as my very own. You are My irreplaceable bride, My royal diadem. A crown of great beauty, poised through the hands of time, extravagant forevermore.

Sue Hodkinson

"My King, I feel silly about You. Quite smitten with my newfound love for You. It's a remarkable place to be. I softly whisper my heart's desire to You, and place Your hand upon my chest that I might impart to You the rhythm of this new song and dance. Search the secret place in my heart, and You will find my love grows more and more receptive of You. I sense the warmth of Your presence over me, as my heart beats with excitement. Come, linger with me awhile. I am so happy You are here!"

A gentle breeze blows, the essence of My love and desire for you. This melody is heard in forte! My love is designed to carry you to the highest heights, and there I shall embrace all that you have for Me.

"You are a love all of my very own! All I think about is You!"

Shall we enter in, My love? Open your heart to Me. Wisdom calls you, answer her. She has words for you; a time and a place just for you. Receive them and come away with Me! I am the light of the world. He that follows Me shall not walk in darkness, but shall have the light of life. Will you respond to My voice when I speak so firmly and passionately over you? I will hold your place before Me while you prepare yourself to accompany Me. You will respond to Me with gesture, and with great reward. Are you ready for Me, My love?

Sue Hodkinson

"My heart beats with excitement because You are close. Draw me away! With words I adore You, my heart embraces You! Yes, I am Yours! There is but one God, the Father from whom all things came, and through whom we live, and there is but one Lord Jesus Christ, through whom all things came and through whom we live. You are the God who sees me, for I have now seen the one who sees me!"

And what shall be the order of your day? You shall love the Lord your God with all your heart, My love! You shall serve the Lord with gladness and with all your strength, you shall obey and keep My commands. This is how it shall be.

"I reflect upon the grandeur of Your word and its statues during the quiet times. Your excellence speaks for itself, and the quality of its dimensions are an emporium well preserved."

With one stroke of My hand, you will make everything beautiful. I will spread your wings before Me. You will fly up and over the Mountain of the Lord, where you shall return time and time again to the hand of God so near thy dwelling. I shall keep you under the shadow of My wing where you will be nurtured and protected. I will feed you manna from heaven, and adorn you with the fervor of the Lord. My eyes will watch over you day and night while in flight. Your foot shall not slip upon the high places you shall travel, where rocks cut in jagged edge!

"My King, Luke 11:9-10 says: "Ask and it will be given, seek and you will find, knock and the door will be opened to you." Inspire my creativity, O' Great One on High! You are my life, my sacred ambition!"

Sue Hodkinson

My love, let's celebrate our hearts' newest expression! The Kingdom of Heaven is like a treasure hidden in a field. When a man found it, he hid it again, and then in his joy went and sold all he had, and bought that field. Again, the Kingdom of Heaven is like a merchant looking for fine pearls. When he found one of great value, he went away, and sold everything he had, and bought it." *(*Matthew 12:44-45*)* We are going to play hide-n-seek! Search the depth of your heart through each rise and fall of our passion. I want you to find Me like a "treasure hidden in a field, or a merchant looking for fine pearls." You will seek Me and find Me when you seek Me with all your heart. It is the Glory of God to conceal a matter, but the glory of kings is to search it out. Respond to Me, and we shall bring to a climax our love song's serenade!

"My King, Psalm 139: 9-10 says: "If I rise on the wings of the morning, if I settle on the far side of the sea, even there Your hand will guide me, Your right hand will hold me fast—You are inviting, and I am responsive. Bid me come, and I will abandon myself to you as my gift. A gift that opens the way for the giver, and ushers me into the presence of greatness!"

Sue Hodkinson

Song of Solomon 3:2

"I will rise now and go about the city streets
and in the broad ways, I will seek Him whom my soul loveth.
I sought Him, but I found Him not.
Night descends!
O' breaking heart!
My tears will fall, and I shall find no rest!

May I Have This Dance?

"My King! What shall this be between us, a memory in song or is this love alive? Is there a response and does the melody repeat for everlasting effects and impression? What shall this be between us, O' love of my heart? How do I play for thee, O' Great One so near? In solo or with serenade, or shall I play with cymbals to clash loud and strong? What shall this be between us? I come to our garden alone. I sit amongst the lilies, despairing over the passions of this tempo, the sting of its embrace, the shadows of its sorrow. How can this be? How can I survive here alone? So compelling a melody such as this is difficult to bear. I am awakened for you as each moment passes. I call out to thee, silence fills the air! I pray thee, hold me—shelter me. Words cannot express the torment of loss I shall endure. Nay, there are none to compare of the rhapsody I have shared with you!"

Sue Hodkinson

Open your eyes, and wipe those tears away. I am knocking! Can't you hear Me? You are moving ever so slowly to the beat of My heart. As we approach the morning hour, My love, you must keep up the pace. I smell your fragrance; I sense your movement. Open the chamber of your heart to Me!

"My King, I yearn to bathe myself in the estuary of Your Spirit, knowing Your comfort will shower peace to my soul. The flowers of our garden are eternally rich with color. I stroke each one, admiring their beauty in the sunlight. In my thoughts, I caress Your face, and kiss Your cheek. Our love's stanza endures forever!

You believe I have abandoned you to ruin and despair. You believe amiss. Your tears cloud your vision. I am dancing in the midst of your tears! I am singing over thee in the wee hours of the morning. Yes, the light in your heart is dim. I am its flame! Kindle Me! Ignite your passion for Me, and its brightness will return!

"My King, add more oil to my lamp that the light becomes brighter! I want to behold your face more clearly. I want to see the color of Your eyes. Your hair is likened to embroidered threads interwoven in gold. You are a stealth warrior. Your shoulders are firm and strong. You are the most excellent of Kings! My heart is stirred by Your beauty, and the majesty of Your truth!

Sue Hodkinson

My King, add more oil to my lamp that the light becomes brighter! I see the horseman and Your carriage. I see the contour of Your ivory coach, and the splendor of each wheel as You enter the temple courts made ready for its King! Direct my eyes to Your Throne! I want to gaze upon Your brilliance. I want to examine the Scepter of Justice; embrace the majesty of Your service, smell the fragrance of Your robe!

My King, add more oil to my lamp that the light becomes brighter! By day, You direct Your love over me. At night, Your song is with me. I wish to enter into the gates of the temple. I hear the tambourine, and the lyre, and its procession of music. Respond to my invitation!

Open! Open! Open to me thy temple gate, and bid me come to You!"

The simplicity of your heart creates a silhouette of light summoned by the Master's hand. Receive Me that I may obtain from you that which must be. A bestowing, My love, an eternal call for all to see and behold! I have hidden you from this world. What an invigorating feeling of success. You do not hasten to leave the nest I have provided for you. You linger, and yet linger awhile. You embrace Me with your heart, and now with your soul. Your thoughts worship Me; you love Me like a King! Fly High, My love, straight to Me!

"How lovely is your dwelling place, O' Lord Almighty! My heart and my flesh cry out for the living God. Even the sparrow has found a home, and the swallow a nest for herself, where she may have her young. A place near your altar, O' Lord Almighty, my King and my God!"

Sue Hodkinson

Love is having passionate affection for My bride, and creating the object of such affection with her. Look for Me in all you do. I am your first love, and you, My love, are My bride. Choose Me!

"It is You, my King! It is You! I love the warmth that You spread over me, the blue skies in a rainy day, and how the sunshine brilliantly reflects the ardor of our love. I love the laughter that bubbles up from within me when we play together, and the gracelets that fall through heaven's gates to dangle over my head, ready to burst at any moment. You are the minutes in my entire day; the candles lit by the evening's firelight. You possess my heart with all its many melodies, and when You scold me, with tears in my eyes, I listen to You. I love you! It is as if I speak through the airwaves of time. It is You, my King! It is You!"

What is this I am feeling coming straight out of the chamber of your heart? What a wonderful delicate delight! I sense a passionate embrace of motion liken unto the waves of the sea. With open arms, I will greet you as you frolic around Me. I will send you a cool, refreshing breeze. Behold! A new season bearing sounds of your laughter is begun! New colors of green and blue to enhance the desires of My heart!

"My Lord, our song has thoughts that speak to Me. Its melody is pleasant. Each word moves upon my heart to say and do its every command. The sound of our harmony emulates the seriousness of our commitment. Sounds heard in forte, sequenced with acoustics in part. A cry, a call, one of a special tone. I shall listen to the tone of Your voice as I enhance Your movement upon my soul. You fill me with great pleasure! Yes, I am moved!"

Sue Hodkinson

Song of Solomon 7:10

"I am my beloved's and His desire is toward me!"

Come hither, My love! I shall lift thee ever so high upon the crest of our love as the wind of My Spirit embraces you. "May I have this dance with you?" We shall dance to the rhythm of a waltz. First to the left and then to the right.

"He passionately takes my hands in His and firmly and securely places me before Him."

Glide—step—glide, My love! Glide—step—glide! I am the burning bush, and you are My flame! We shall move ever so slowly, emulating the excitement and joy as you pivot in sequence. Back and forth we are suspended in mid-air, creating our own lyrics, basking in the moment, fulfilling our every expectation—yet the threshold of all that unites us together!

Sue Hodkinson

"See me dance, my Lord! Behold, my joy! A sweet smelling fragrance, its laughter pouring out from within me, bubbling up to greet thee on high! So often you touch me tenderly, "I'm free", I shout, "I'm free"! Free to love, free to give, free to be me! See our garden, my Lord? The flowers are all in a row. Gladness fills my heart. I shall pick one for You, and place it in Your hand one day. A gift to You, my Lord, for giving back Your breath of life in me!"

You have given this dance exclusively to Me. I receive it, My love, and its fragrance is sublime!

"I love you! I love you! Each receptive heartbeat reflects this passion of our love, together with the season of time. You have embraced me, carried me, nurtured me, and kept me! Do not hide from me the light of Your word, and the reflection of its influence upon my life. You inspire me to savor the love which we share."

I shall always respond to you!

"O' what a great abundance of peace! I sing for joy as You bring the wildflowers to my table and warm my heart with the serenity of Your presence. You lavished upon me gifts of the circumcised, and with open arms, I received them one, and all! The fragrant calamus was planted in my garden where the stream of living waters flows! I enjoy You, My King, and am set apart just for You. You are my hero sent from afar. The Prince in my life who blankets my eternal soul! Now, and forevermore, it is I who humbly rejoices over You!"

Sue Hodkinson

My love, I am enchanted by you. We have accomplished a time and a place between us. An orchestra of notes, a rhyme carried over through time, and melodies spoken.

"Come, sit beside me. Take my hand; it's Yours! Everything is perfect now that we are together. Tears of joy stream down my face. I'm home! It's as You said, My King: "The moments pass as life begins, and life begins with You!"

Song of Solomon 2:4
"He has taken me to the banquet hall,
and His banner over me is love!"

Sue Hodkinson

"I take You, My King, as my all-in-all. To live, and to love You in sickness and in health. To have and to hold the essence of who I am in You. To serve You with a heart of gladness in Your Kingdom's Glory as I endeavor to rebuild and to restore, imparting to the world Your merciful grace and its truth therein."

Welcome home, My love! There is a bride, and there is a Bridegroom. The church is made ready. The event in waiting. Consider, if you will, all the preparatory measures taken to ensure success. Not by one, My love, but by two. Understand if you will, this medley is a musical piece made up of various tunes and passages liken unto a spinet—all created by you and me.

May I Have This Dance?

"I have come to the Mountain of the Lord where you have stolen my heart! Its countryside is perfumed with the fragrance of myrrh and incense, as the well of living waters flows freely upon the garden of my life—on this, the day of my betrothal, the day my heart rejoices over you!"

Our song began at the beginning; its tempo was fixed and secured. The passions of our heart created this final sanction. Believe in all that we are, and what we are experiencing is genuine. Acknowledge if you will, the invitations have been sent, and the guests have all arrived. The banquet table is eloquently prepared for you, and I myself will make a feast of rich foods, and wine aged with time.

Sue Hodkinson

"The banquet table is set and ready for consumption. You have summoned Your carriage to escort me to Your chamber door. The musicians have arrived. I am clothed in a garment of salvation and arrayed with a robe of righteousness. You are a gentleman and a scholar of Your word. I will delight greatly in You, My King, and in my faithfulness, You shall reward me according to your riches in glory!"

The church is made ready, My love! The hour spontaneous, the timing made perfect. You will find Me as I stand at the altar in expectation of you to come down the aisle. My eye is ever fixed in search of you—for that sudden glimpse of you as you make way into the reality of My world. My heart is pounding as we seize the moment, and time stands still just for us. You shall come forth to Me, and I shall embrace you in My arms.

"I take you, My King, as my blazing spiritual torch, manifesting a light to radiate into my life the beauty of your wisdom and truth. I am the redeemed of the Lord. I will be a crown of splendor in my Savior's hand. A royal diadem in the hand of my King!"

May I kiss you, My love? A greeting marked with passionate affection! You are beautifully embellished as My bride. As a loosely flowing gown, My grace is ever upon you. I hear your heart singing over Me. There is a sparkle, a gleam in your eyes. Your smile is radiant as your laughter fills the air. My sentiments exactly, My love!

Sue Hodkinson

"I take you, My King, as the noblest of all warriors. Experienced in battle, and robed with honor as a watchman on my walls. You call forth thy sword, a signal to defeat the terrors of my night, and yet enforce the liberties of my days. We shall unite, My King, as the many waters that connect near the banks of the river's edge to become one thriving impregnable stream! I am dressed in full armor! I am in love!"

I will adorn you with honor and esteem. Ornaments to wear around your neck, My love. Precious jewels of prosperity, and distinction to shine upon you with a heavenly glow! You shall step into the fullness of My joy, and pleasures forevermore!

"You are my Father, my God, Jesus Christ, my Savior and King! I will maintain my love to You forever, and my covenant with You shall never fail. I will establish Your throne forever, as long as the heavens endure, according to Psalms 89: 28-29. This is my everlasting promise to You!

I shall take you as My bride, and I shall become your all-in-all! You will enter My rest I have prepared for you. You are a cascade of waterfall colors arranged to frame My world with the sweetness of your fragrance!

I am the Artist who creates such beauty as this! I am the Caretaker of the universe! Capture My rhythm and design—an intricate flourish of cascade in motion!

www.ingramcontent.com/pod-product-compliance
Lightning Source LLC
Chambersburg PA
CBHW041959080526
44588CB00021B/2809